ELMHURST PUBLIC LIBRARY

3 1135 01740 0224

W9-AUQ-030

FRANKLIN PUBLIC LIBRARY
MEDIA CENTER
FRANKLIN, WISCONSIN

— MONSTER WARS —

VAMPIRES VS. WEREWOLVES

BATTLE OF THE BLOODTHIRSTY BEASTS

by Michael O'Hearn

Consultant:
Michael Delahoyde, PhD
Washington State University
Pullman, Washington

ELMHURST PUBLIC LIBRARY
125 S. Prospect Avenue
Elmhurst, IL 60126-3298

CAPSTONE PRESS
a capstone imprint

Edge Books are published by Capstone Press,
151 Good Counsel Drive, P.O. Box 669, Mankato, Minnesota 56002.
www.capstonepub.com

Copyright © 2012 by Capstone Press, a Capstone imprint.
All rights reserved.
No part of this publication may be reproduced in whole or in part,
or stored in a retrieval system, or transmitted in any form or by any means,
electronic, mechanical, photocopying, recording, or otherwise, without
written permission of the publisher.
For information regarding permission, write to Capstone Press,
151 Good Counsel Drive, P.O. Box 669, Dept. R, Mankato, Minnesota 56002.

Books published by Capstone Press are manufactured with paper
containing at least 10 percent post-consumer waste.

Library of Congress Cataloging-in-Publication Data
O'Hearn, Michael, 1972–
    Vampires vs. werewolves : battle of the bloodthirsty beasts / by Michael O'Hearn.
    p. cm.—(Edge books. Monster wars)
    Summary: "Describes the features and abilities of vampires and werewolves, and
how they may battle each other in a fight"—Provided by publisher.
    Includes bibliographical references and index.
    ISBN 978-1-4296-6521-6 (library binding)
    ISBN 978-1-4296-7265-8 (paperback)
    1. Vampires—Juvenile literature. 2. Werewolves—Juvenile literature.
I. Title. II. Series.
BF1556.O54 2012
398'.45—dc22   2011003784

Editorial Credits
Aaron Sautter, editor; Tracy Davies, designer; Eric Gohl, media researcher;
    Eric Manske, production specialist

Illustrations
McLean Kendree

Photo Credits
Alamy/Moviestore Collection Ltd, 9 (top); Photos 12, 5 (top), 6 (left),
    11, 17 (bottom)
Getty Images Inc./Tim Flach, 14
iStockphoto/Paula Goulart (vampire & werewolf silhouette)
Newscom/akg-images, 12; Beitia Archives, 17 (top); Hollywood Pictures/
    Stonewood.com, 15; Universal Pictures, 5 (bottom), 13; Universal Pictures/
    Parent/Stuber, 6 (right), 10, 19 (left); Warner Brothers, 19 (right)
Shutterstock/javarman, 9 (bottom)

Printed in the United States of America in Steves Point, Wisconsin.
032011   006111WZF11

TABLE OF CONTENTS

J
398.45
O'He

WELCOME TO MONSTER WARS!

It's past midnight. The night is dark. Shadows creep across your bedroom wall. You swear they form a slit-eyed face. Floorboards creak. Trees outside your window groan. It's nothing, you tell yourself. But you lie awake … watching … listening … waiting. You can't help but think a terrifying monster is hiding in your closet.

In these pages, you'll learn the strengths and weaknesses of vampires and werewolves. And you'll see them clash in a monstrous battle. Will the vampire be able to defeat the vicious werewolf? Or will the werewolf's fury help him escape the vampire's deadly bite?

Are monsters real? No. But be ready for a legendary bloody battle.

THE FRIGHTENING TRUTH:

VAMPIRE VS. WEREWOLF

The most famous tales of blood-sucking vampires come from Eastern Europe. During the 1200s, vampire hunters sometimes investigated unexplained deaths. They dug up graves to look for evidence of vampire activity. Sometimes dead bodies decay slowly. Some fresh bodies may look as if they're still alive. Vampire hunters often thought these bodies were vampires that caused unexplained sickness and death.

Werewolves are also known for their bloodthirsty nature. In many tales, werewolves feed on farm animals. But in others, they attack people. These creatures are cursed men, often controlled by the power of the moon.

People in Europe once thought werewolves were real monsters. During the 1500s, when a brutal killing occurred, men were sometimes put on trial for being werewolves. Some of these men were accused because they looked strange and made people uncomfortable. Others were simply in the wrong place at the wrong time. Even with little evidence, many of these men were put to death.

Which of these legendary creatures of the night would you rather avoid under the full moon? Read on to learn their bloody secrets!

SHAPE-SHIFTING POWERS

Some werewolves change into wolflike beasts by using magical animal **pelts** or creams. In French and German legends, these magical items were gifts from the devil. These werewolves could choose when to unleash their savage powers.

Other werewolves are cursed to become a fierce beast under the glow of a full moon. It's impossible to know who carries this curse until it's too late. These werewolves can pass the curse on to others with a bite—assuming their victims survive the attack.

Vampires are also able to change their shape. They can turn into bats, wolves, or even misty fog. A vampire may change its appearance to **deceive** its victims. The creature may appear as a relative or a lover. The victim has no reason to be afraid, making it easy for the vampire to attack.

VAMPIRE changes own shape
★★★★★

WEREWOLF changes by moonlight
★★★

pelt — an animal's skin with hair or fur still on it

deceive — to trick or fool someone

SPEED

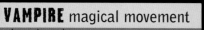

VAMPIRE magical movement
★ ★ ★

WEREWOLF fast, nimble runner
★ ★ ★ ★ ★

Werewolves **stalk** their prey before attacking. They can blend into the shadows and cut quickly through dense forests. Werewolves have very strong legs. They can leap great distances and land with perfect balance. They are sure-footed, nimble runners. They can spring upon their victims and attack with deadly speed.

stalk — to hunt in a quiet, secret way

When in physical form, vampires move only as fast as their shape allows. But vampires often move in magical ways. In the story *Dracula*, vampires can turn into mist and fly through the air. Floating on the wind, they can slip through open windows and slide through key holes. In a few legends, vampires can enter a person's dreams, even from a great distance. These vampires can be as deadly to sleeping victims as they are to those who are awake.

FRIGHTFUL FACT

Bram Stoker's *Dracula* was inspired by the Romanian ruler Vlad Tepes. Tepes was known for impaling his enemies on long, spiked poles. These terrible acts earned him the nickname "Vlad the Impaler."

INTELLIGENCE

VAMPIRE superior knowledge

★ ★ ★ ★

WEREWOLF strong instincts

★ ★ ★

Vampires may be the smartest of all monsters. They can live for thousands of years. Living so long allows them to gain a great deal of knowledge. Vampires are **cunning** and single-minded in their desires. They don't care who gets hurt to get what they want. Vampires' thirst for blood, combined with their high intelligence, make them especially dangerous monsters.

Werewolves are as smart as humans. Although they lack the knowledge of vampires, they make up for it with strong **instincts**. Werewolves are naturally skilled hunters. They know how to find victims. They can sniff out victims with ease, and they know the best place and time to attack. With a mix of human intelligence and animal instinct, werewolves are extremely deadly.

FRIGHTFUL FACT

Wolves have tails, but werewolves do not.

cunning — clever
instinct — behavior that is natural

ATTACK STYLE

VAMPIRE cunning killer
★ ★ ★

WEREWOLF fierce and bloody
★ ★ ★ ★ ★

Vampires are armed with intelligence, charm, and deadly fangs. They lure their victims close before they strike. They may shape-shift into a friendly or familiar person. They may put a victim into a trance. Or they might sneak up on a sleeping person as mist. When they're close, vampires attack with their sharp fangs. The monsters can quickly suck a victim dry of blood.

A werewolf's sharp teeth and powerful jaws easily tear flesh from bone. Werewolves have supernatural strength and an overpowering hunger for flesh. At the first taste of blood, a werewolf becomes more vicious in its attack. Werewolves don't think during battle. Their beastly instincts take over. They simply strike, wound, and kill.

FRIGHTFUL FACT

Vampires have superhuman strength in many books and movies.

WEAKNESSES

Killing a vampire requires great bravery. In most stories, driving a wooden stake through the monster's heart is the best way to make sure it's dead. In some tales, vampire hunters chop up the body and burn it too. The sun is also deadly to vampires. The monsters sleep in coffins to hide from the sun during the day. Exposing a vampire to direct sunlight might also get the job done.

Some stories say werewolves can die any way a normal wolf can. In other legends, a sharp object made of silver can kill the beast, or at least return it to human form. In modern tales, the surest way to kill a werewolf is with a silver bullet. But the first shot needs to count. The savage monster would quickly attack anyone who tried to shoot it more than once.

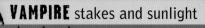

VAMPIRE stakes and sunlight
★★★

WEREWOLF silver bullets
★★★

FRIGHTFUL FACT

Legends say that holy water and crucifixes can injure vampires. Garlic hung in doorways is also said to keep vampires away.

GET READY TO RUMBLE!

When you hear a blood-curdling howl under the full moon, you'll know the battle is on! The savage werewolf is wild and hungry. The blood-thirsty vampire is crafty and cunning. After this battle in the dead of night, one creature will never taste blood again. The other will feast and live to continue its reign of terror.

Keep out of the dark woods at night, but don't stop reading. You've got a full-moon view of this monstrous battle. It's a clash between a wily bloodsucker and a vicious beast!

The werewolf growls viciously. The vampire smiles thinly and laughs. Without warning, the werewolf leaps forward—his fang-filled mouth wide open. His arms, not quite wolf and not quite human, stretch out as if to tackle the vampire. But at the moment of impact, the vampire is gone. A dark, leathery bat hovers in its place.

The werewolf stops and turns. It growls at the bat, which flaps its wings and disappears into the darkness.

The werewolf raises its muzzle and sniffs the air. It catches its enemy's scent and darts into the forest. The beast's dark fur flutters in the wind as it bounds between the trees. It moves with speed and certainty. The hunt is on!

Finally, the beast reaches a clearing. It moves forward slowly, hunched low to the ground. Just ahead, the vampire stands beside a crumbling stone castle.

The werewolf howls insanely. It scrapes at the ground with its sharp claws. It tightens its jaws and growls through its sharp, deadly teeth.

The vampire stares intently at the beast. He tries to control its mind, to force the beast to be silent and still. A calm creature will be easy to kill. But the werewolf lacks a human mind. It is too animal-like to be controlled by the vampire's power.

Unfazed, the werewolf crouches low, and then launches itself at the vampire. It opens its powerful jaws wide to strike. It streaks through the air and collides with its enemy. The fierce beast sinks its teeth deep in its enemy's flesh.

With the taste of blood in its mouth, the werewolf strikes out savagely. It throws the vampire to the ground. It slashes its sharp claws at the fallen foe. It clamps its powerful jaws down once again on the vampire's cold flesh.

The werewolf's eyes blaze. It growls and howls. Then it grabs hold of his enemy with long fingers and flings him against a thick tree. The vampire impacts sharply and crashes to the dirt.

The werewolf is upon him. It smells blood and death. It strikes again and again. It raises its mad eyes to the moon and howls. Blood and drool drip from its jaws. Then a red mist rises, and the vampire is gone.

The werewolf stops and sniffs the air. Baffled, it stares into the dark woods.

Then a twig snaps. The beast leaps toward the trees. There among the shadows stands the pale, bloody vampire. Something thin and sharp glints between his fingers. The werewolf springs onto his enemy once again. His deadly teeth bite into the bloodsucker's cold flesh.

The vampire glares at the beast clinging to his shoulder. Blood pours from his wounds, but he doesn't flinch. Between his fingers he holds a silver pin. He raises his free arm and pricks the werewolf's neck.

Suddenly, the ferocious beast drops to the ground. It groans and squirms. Its flesh lightens. Its muzzle shrinks. Thick hair slides back into its body. A normal man lies there now, dirty and bloody.

The vampire crouches beside him. He leans forward and sinks his fangs into the man's neck. He laughs wickedly as he drains the warm blood from his victim.

GLOSSARY

crucifix (KROO-suh-fix)—a symbol of the beliefs of Christians

cunning (KUHN-ing)—intelligent and clever at tricking people

deceive (di-SEEV)—to play a trick or lie to make someone believe something that is not true

impale (im-PALE)—to thrust a sharpened stake through a person's body

instinct (IN-stingkt)—behavior that is natural rather than learned

muzzle (MUHZ-uhl)—an animal's nose, mouth, and jaws

pelt (PELT)—an animal's skin with the hair or fur still on it

stalk (STAWK)—to hunt in a quiet, secret way

trance (TRANSS)—a conscious state where someone is not aware of what is happening

READ MORE

Gee, Joshua. *Encyclopedia Horrifica: The Terrifying Truth about Vampires, Ghosts, Monsters and More.* New York: Scholastic, Inc., 2007.

Krensky, Stephen. *Vampires.* Monster Chronicles. Minneapolis, Minn.: Lerner Publications, 2007.

Krensky, Stephen. *Werewolves.* Monster Chronicles. Minneapolis, Minn.: Lerner Publications, 2007.

INTERNET SITES

FactHound offers a safe, fun way to find Internet sites related to this book. All of the sites on FactHound have been researched by our staff.

Here's all you do:

Visit *www.facthound.com*

Type in this code: 9781429665216

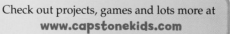

Super-cool stuff!

Check out projects, games and lots more at
www.capstonekids.com

INDEX